Dakota

# GROSS BUGS

# Mosquitoes

Jonathan Kravetz

The Rosen Publishing Group's

## PowerKids Press™

New York

*To Jake, Sam, and Kyra*

Published in 2006 by The Rosen Publishing Group, Inc.
29 East 21st Street, New York, NY 10010

First Edition

Editor: Jennifer Way
Book Design: Ginny Chu

Photo Credits: Cover © CDC/PHIL/Corbis; p. 5 Darwin Dale/Photo Researchers, Inc.; p. 6 © David Muench/Corbis; p. 9 © Bettmann/Corbis; p. 10 © Richard T. Nowitz/Corbis; p. 13 G. I. Bernard/Photo Researchers, Inc.; p. 14 (left) © Clouds Hill Imaging Ltd/Corbis; p. 14 (right) Sinclair Stammers/Photo Researchers, Inc.; p. 17 Martin Dohrn/Photo Researchers, Inc.; p. 18 David M. Schleser/Nature's Images/Photo Researchers, Inc.; p. 21 © Charles Krebs/Corbis.

Library of Congress Cataloging-in-Publication Data

Kravetz, Jonathan.
  Mosquitoes / Jonathan Kravetz.— 1st ed.
      p. cm. — (Gross bugs)
  Includes index.
  ISBN 1-4042-3044-0 (library binding)
  1.  Mosquitoes–Juvenile literature.  I. Title.

  QL536.K76 2006
  595.77'2—dc22
                                              2004025426

Manufactured in the United States of America

# CONTENTS

# The Deadliest Insect

The mosquito is one of the deadliest animals on Earth. When mosquitoes feed on human blood, these tiny **insects** can spread **diseases**, such as malaria. Even today more than one million people around the world die from malaria each year. Most mosquitoes are from ⅛ to ¼ of an inch long (3–6 mm). They have thin bodies, with two thin **antennae**, and a long, tubelike mouth, called a **proboscis**.

Mosquitoes belong to a **family** of insects called Culicidae. There are around 2,700 different **species** of mosquitoes spread all over Earth and around 150 species in the United States. Mosquitoes are related to gnats and flies. Flies, mosquitoes, and gnats are all part of a larger **order** called Diptera, which means "two wings."

In this picture of a female mosquito, you can see that her body is swollen with the blood she has sucked, and her two sets of wings are spread. The word "mosquito" is Spanish for "little fly." People have tried many ways to kill mosquitoes, but they, and the diseases they spread, continue to be a problem in many parts of the world.

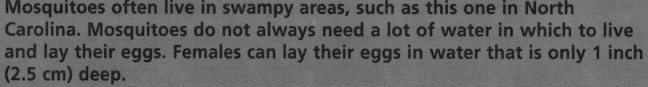

Mosquitoes often live in swampy areas, such as this one in North Carolina. Mosquitoes do not always need a lot of water in which to live and lay their eggs. Females can lay their eggs in water that is only 1 inch (2.5 cm) deep.

# A Swampy Home

Mosquitoes live near standing water because that is where female mosquitoes lay their eggs. Mosquito **larvae** and **pupae** also live and grow in standing water. These areas of standing water can include ponds and swamps. Some mosquitoes live in areas heavily populated by people and will **mate** in the standing water collected in clogged gutters, cans, birdbaths, and swimming pools. Although mosquitoes are usually found in warm places on Earth, there have even been mosquitoes found in cold places such as Siberia!

Millions of years ago, mosquitoes were bigger than they are today. The mosquito's proboscis was smaller. The small proboscis made it hard for it to suck blood. Over time the mosquito changed. The proboscis grew much longer, which made it easier for the mosquito to drink blood. At the same time, its body got smaller.

# What Mosquitoes Look Like

Like all insects mosquitoes' bodies are divided into three parts. These are the head, **thorax**, and **abdomen**. The mosquito's head has two antennae and two eyes. Mosquitoes have poor eyesight, but their eyes help them to balance themselves while they fly. The female mosquito's mouth, or proboscis, looks like a long tube. The female uses this to pierce, or cut into, skin and feed on blood. Males use their proboscis to feed on flower nectar.

The mosquito has two wings on its thorax. Also connected to the thorax are six legs, each with a pair of tiny claws, which the mosquito uses to hold onto surfaces.

The mosquito's abdomen is where its stomach is located. If you see a female mosquito who has just eaten, you can see her abdomen swollen with the blood meal.

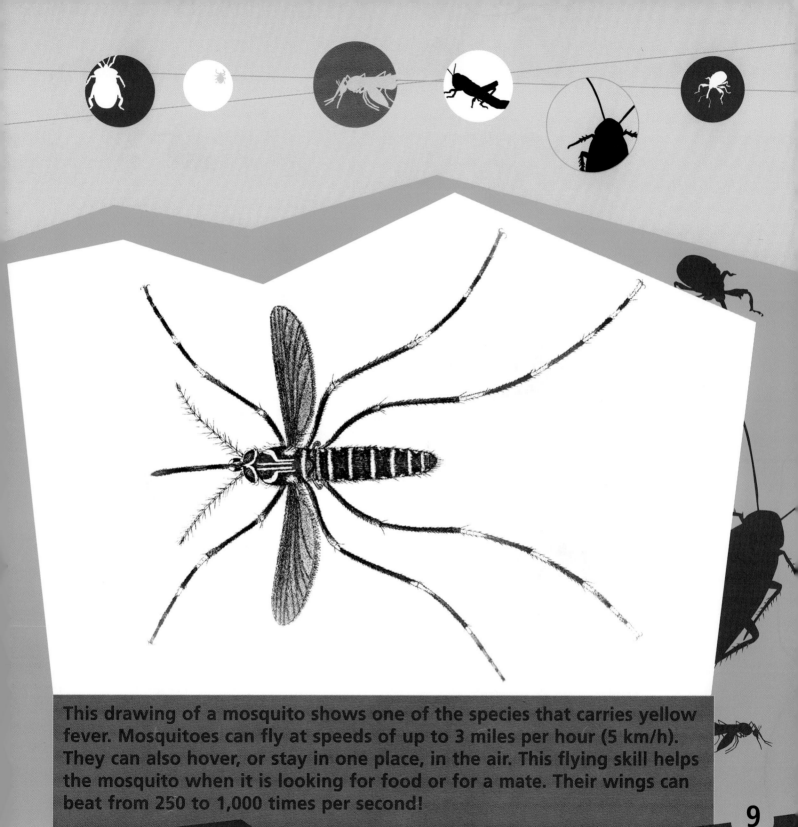

This drawing of a mosquito shows one of the species that carries yellow fever. Mosquitoes can fly at speeds of up to 3 miles per hour (5 km/h). They can also hover, or stay in one place, in the air. This flying skill helps the mosquito when it is looking for food or for a mate. Their wings can beat from 250 to 1,000 times per second!

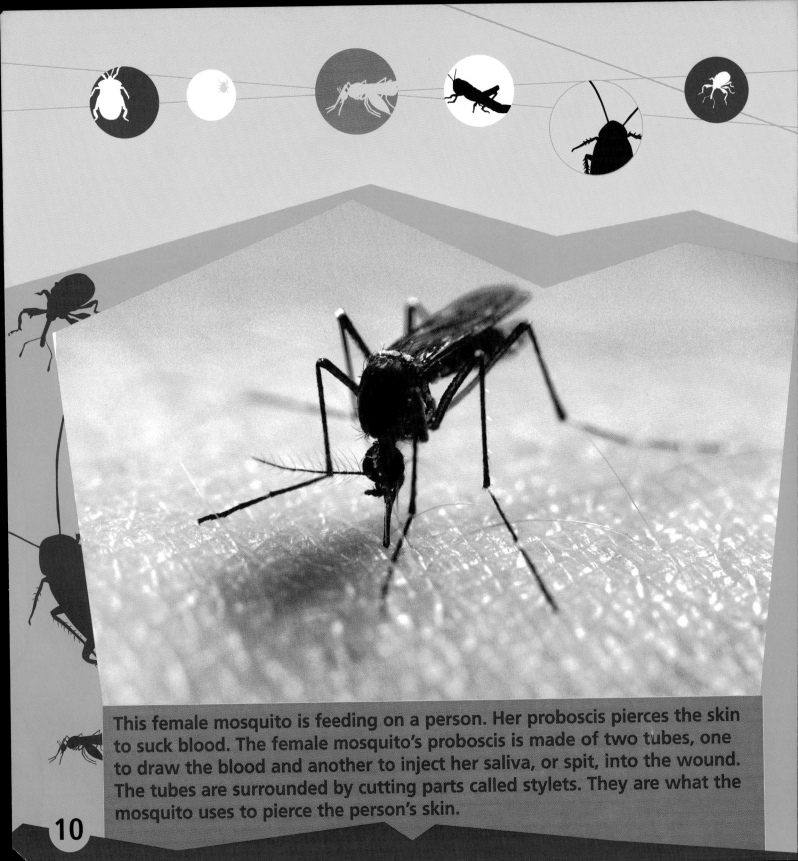

This female mosquito is feeding on a person. Her proboscis pierces the skin to suck blood. The female mosquito's proboscis is made of two tubes, one to draw the blood and another to inject her saliva, or spit, into the wound. The tubes are surrounded by cutting parts called stylets. They are what the mosquito uses to pierce the person's skin.

# What Mosquitoes Eat and What Eats Them

Only some mosquito species feed on human blood. In fact only the females of these species drink blood. The **nutrients** in blood help females produce eggs. Male mosquitoes eat nectar and other sources of sugar, such as rotting fruit. Female mosquitoes also eat these things when they are not producing eggs.

When a female mosquito finds an animal to feed on, she lands on its skin. The female mosquito then uses her proboscis to find a place to draw blood. When female mosquitoes bite, they inject some of their saliva into the wound. This causes the wound to swell up and itch.

Many types of animals eat mosquitoes. These animals include fish, insects, reptiles, birds, and amphibians.

# The Beginning

Mosquitoes undergo four stages in their lives. These stages are egg, larva, pupa, and adult. The changing between states is called **metamorphosis**. The egg is the first of these stages.

After a female mosquito mates, she rests for a few days to allow the eggs inside her to grow. This is an unsafe time for her and her eggs, because it is easier for animals that eat mosquitoes to catch and eat the resting female.

After she has rested, the female lays her eggs in standing water. She lands on the surface of the water and lowers her abdomen into the water to lay the eggs. The eggs are laid in a group that forms a floating raft. The eggs can hatch in as few as two days. The egg raft can sometimes live through winter and hatch the next spring.

This is a side view of a mosquito egg raft floating on top of the water. Females can lay up to 250 eggs in an egg raft. Most females only live long enough to mate once in their lives.

13

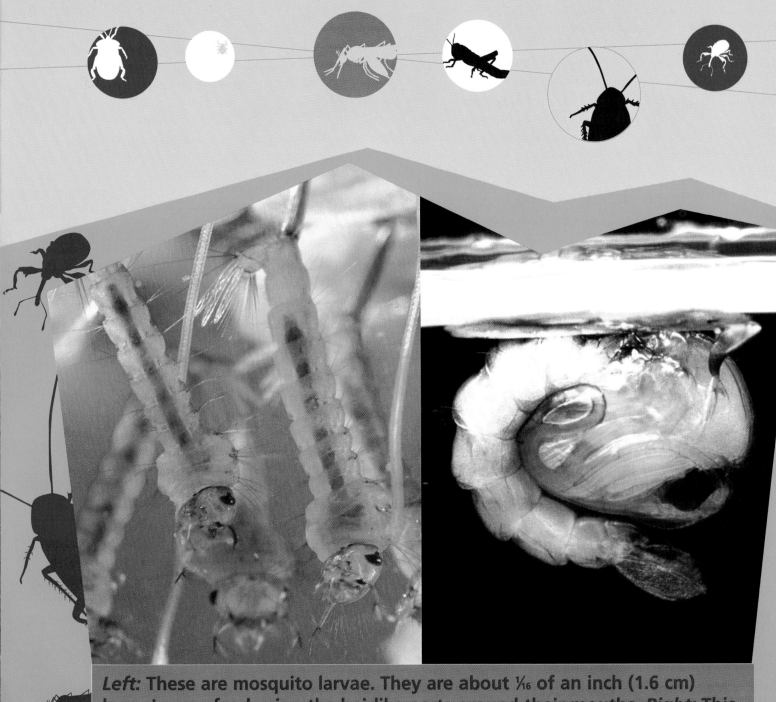

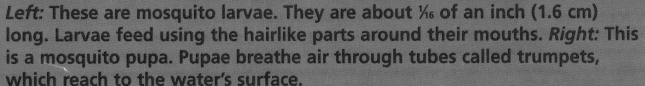

*Left:* These are mosquito larvae. They are about ¹⁄₁₆ of an inch (1.6 cm) long. Larvae feed using the hairlike parts around their mouths. *Right:* This is a mosquito pupa. Pupae breathe air through tubes called trumpets, which reach to the water's surface.

# Wrigglers and Tumblers

When the egg hatches, a grayish white larva comes out of the egg. Mosquito larvae are called wrigglers because of how they squirm in the water. Larvae eat mostly **microorganisms** found in the water. The larvae feed continuously so that they can grow. As a wriggler grows, it sheds its skin. This is called **molting**. The number of molts a larva undergoes depends on the species.

After the final molt, mosquito larvae enter the pupal stage. Pupae also live in the water, but they do not eat. They have a strong outer skin, called the pupal case. Pupae sense movement and tumble to get away from danger. This is why they are called tumblers. Pupae soon grow into adult mosquitoes. This takes from one to four days, depending on the species and the weather.

# Adults

When the pupal stage comes to an end, the adult mosquito swallows air to puff itself up and break open the pupal case. The adult then rests on the water. Its skin and wings are soft and it is too weak to fly. After about half an hour, the outer skin hardens and the fully grown mosquito can fly away.

Female mosquitoes can live from a few days to a few weeks. Male mosquitoes usually live only long enough to mate once or twice. This is only about two to four days. How long a mosquito lives also depends on the species and the weather. As mosquitoes age their wings begin to wear out. They might also lose a leg or two. A mosquito that lives an unusually long time might live as long as five or six months.

*Left:* This adult mosquito is pulling itself out of the pupal case. *Right:* After the mosquito comes out of the pupal case, it needs to rest. It is weak, and its wings are not yet strong enough to fly. This is another stage at which it is easier for the mosquito to be caught by an animal that wants to eat it.

This female mosquito is laying her eggs. Although sometimes they live long enough to mate two or three times, most females mate only once. When the eggs have been fertilized, she feeds on a blood meal. The nutrients in one blood meal can help the female produce as many as 250 eggs.

# Mating and Laying Eggs

Within a couple of days of becoming an adult, mosquitoes are ready to mate. The male's antennae are longer and bushier than the female's. This helps him sense the buzzing of a female's wings.

When male mosquitoes are ready to mate, hundreds of them gather. They form a large group, called a swarm, in the air. They meet near a landmark, called a swarm marker. Females then fly into the swarm, one by one. Once one of the males chooses a female, the two mosquitoes fly to the ground and mate. After the male **fertilizes** the female's eggs, he flies away to mate with another female. The female goes in search of a blood meal, so the eggs can grow. An average female mosquito will lay just one group of eggs in her lifetime.

# Spreading Disease

Mosquitoes can carry and spread deadly diseases. Some of these diseases include yellow fever and malaria. Each year more than a million people die from diseases they get from mosquitoes.

The United States has gotten rid of most of the worst mosquito-carried diseases using **pesticides**. Outbreaks still happen, however. In 1999, mosquitoes caused a small outbreak of a disease called the West Nile virus in New York City.

Since the female mosquito feeds on blood, the female is the one that spreads disease. A mosquito can pick up a disease from a person's blood. The disease stays with the mosquito. When the mosquito bites another human, the disease passes into the next person.

As this female mosquito feeds on a human hand, the blood can be seen in her abdomen. If a female drinks blood from a person who has a disease, she can spread it to other people when she injects her saliva into the next person.

# How People Fight Mosquitoes

There are many problems scientists face in trying to fight mosquitoes. Mosquitoes can become resistant to pesticides, which means the pesticides no longer kill them.

There are some easy ways to protect yourself and your home from mosquitoes. Get rid of standing water in your yard so that mosquitoes have nowhere to live or mate. It is also a good idea to wear long sleeves and pants when spending time outdoors. To keep mosquitoes from entering your home, make sure that your window screens do not have holes. Scientists have found many ways to fight mosquitoes and the diseases they spread. However, guarding yourself and your home is an important first step in battling these insects.

# GLOSSARY

**abdomen** (AB-duh-min)  The large, rear part of an insect's body.

**antennae** (an-TEH-nee)  Thin, rodlike organs used to feel things, which are located on the head of certain animals.

**diseases** (dih-ZEEZ-ez)  Illnesses or sicknesses.

**family** (FAM-lee)  The scientific name for a large group of plants or animals that are alike in some ways.

**fertilizes** (FUR-tuh-lyz-ez)  Puts male cells inside an egg to make babies.

**insects** (IN-sekts)  Small creatures that often have six legs and wings.

**larvae** (LAR-vee)  Insects in the early life stage, in which they have a wormlike form.

**mate** (MAYT)  To join together to make babies.

**metamorphosis** (meh-tuh-MOR-fuh-sus)  A complete change in form.

**microorganisms** (my-kroh-OR-guh-nih-zuhmz)  Very tiny living things.

**molting** (MOHLT-ing)  Shedding hair, feathers, shell, horns, or skin.

**nutrients** (NOO-tree-ints)  Food that a living thing needs to live and grow.

**order** (OR-dur)  In biology, a category to classify animals. It ranks above a family and below a class.

**pesticides** (PES-tuh-sydz)  Poisons used to kill pests.

**proboscis** (pruh-BAH-sus)  A tubelike mouthpart that insects use to suck in liquid food.

**pupae** (PYOO-pee)  Insects in the second stage of life, in which they change from larvae to adults.

**species** (SPEE-sheez)  A single kind of living thing. All people are one species.

**thorax** (THOR-aks)  The middle part of the body of an insect.

# INDEX

## A
abdomen, 8, 12
antennae, 4, 8, 19

## C
Culicidae, 4

## D
Diptera, 4

## E
egg(s), 12, 15, 19

## L
larva(e), 7, 12, 15

## M
malaria, 4, 20
metamorphosis, 12
microorganisms, 15
molting, 15

## P
pesticides, 20, 22
proboscis, 4, 8, 11
pupa(e), 7, 12, 15

## S
swarm, 19

## T
thorax, 8

## W
West Nile virus, 20
wings, 4, 8, 16, 19

## Y
yellow fever, 20

## Web Sites
Due to the changing nature of Internet links, PowerKids Press has developed an online list of Web sites related to the subject of this book. This site is updated regularly. Please use this link to access the list:
www.powerkidslinks.com/gbugs/mosquito/